Design a T-shirt fit for this fossil hunter.

So far, scientists have discovered more than 1,000 different kinds of dinosaurs. Can you doodle the dinosaurs shown below?

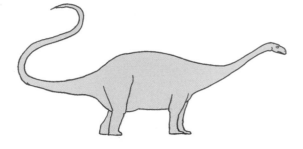

Sauropods were big, plant-eating dinosaurs.

Ceratopsians were horned plant eaters.

Ankylosaurus was a plant-eating dinosaur with heavy armor and spikes.

DINOSAU DOODLES

Andrew Pinder

RP | KIDS
PHILADELPHIA • LONDON

Written and illustrated by
Andrew Pinder

First published in Great Britain by Buster Books,
an imprint of Michael O'Mara Books Limited, 2010

First published in the United States
by Running Press Book Publishers, 2011

Printed in China

9 8 7 6 5 4 3 2 1
Digit on the right indicates the number of this printing

ISBN 978-0-7624-3894-5

Illustrated by Andrew Pinder

This edition published by Running Press Kids,
an imprint of Running Press Book Publishers
2300 Chestnut Street
Philadelphia, PA 19103-4371

Visit us on the web!
www.runningpress.com

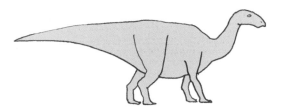

Ornithopods were small
plant eaters.

Theropods were mainly
big meat eaters . . .

. . . but there were also
small **theropods.**

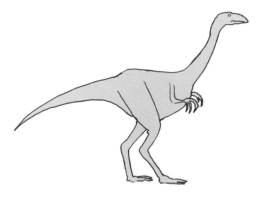

Ornithomimosaurs were
shaped a little like ostriches.

Some dinosaurs had feathers.

Give this dinosaur, named **Deinonychus**, feathers.

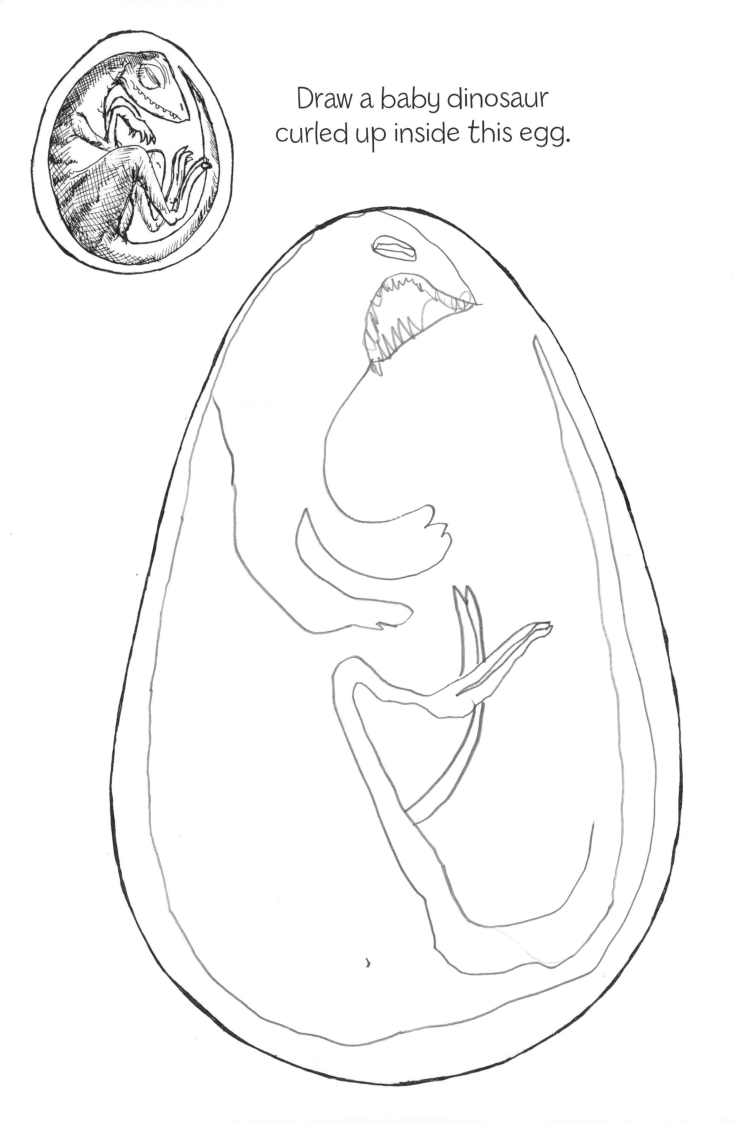

Draw a baby dinosaur
curled up inside this egg.

This is the skull of a **Stygimoloch**.
It had horns and spikes all over
its head.

Draw a head on this Stygimoloch.

Eoraptor was one of the
very first dinosaurs.
It was the size of a chicken.

Draw an Eoraptor chasing this lizard.

Some of the first dinosaurs swallowed stones, which stayed
in their stomachs and helped to grind up
the tough leaves that they ate.

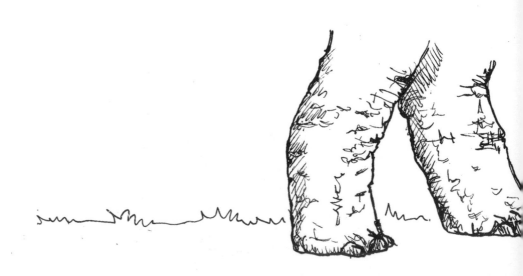

Doodle a dinosaur around these intestines.

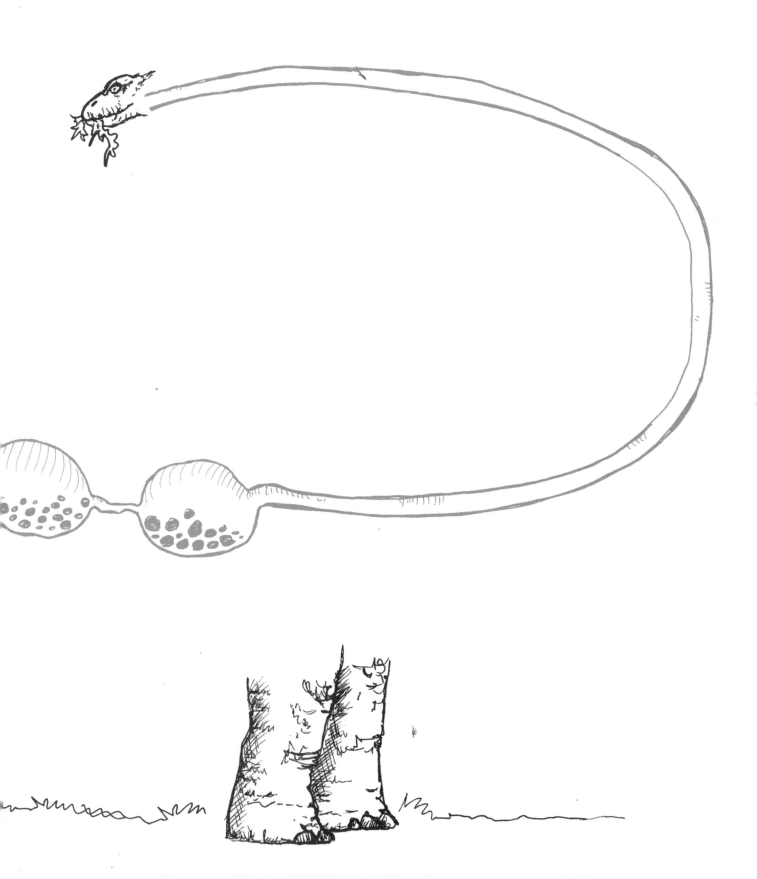

Einiosaurus was a dinosaur that had a huge frill on its head with lots of curly horns on it. It also had a big horn on its nose.

Give this dinosaur horns.

What has hatched out of the eggs of this **Titanosaurus**?

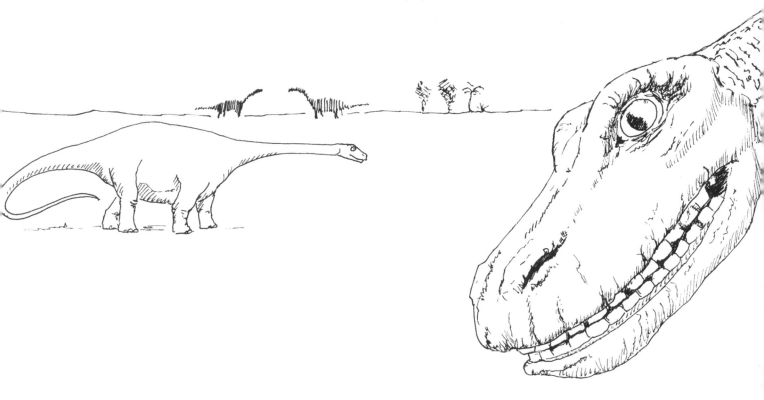

Oviraptors sat on their eggs to keep them warm,
just like birds do today.

Draw lots of Oviraptors on their nests.

This **T-rex** is hungry.

Hide lots of tiny animals in the forest.

Some dinosaurs sank in mud, and millions of years later their fossilized remains were found.

Draw a dinosaur stuck in this swamp.

What is this **T-rex** dreaming about?

Some dinosaurs, such as **Euoplocephalus**, had spikes on their bodies and tails.

Cover this dinosaur's back with spiky armor and give it a heavy club on the end of its tail.

Skulls have helped experts work out what dinosaurs looked like.

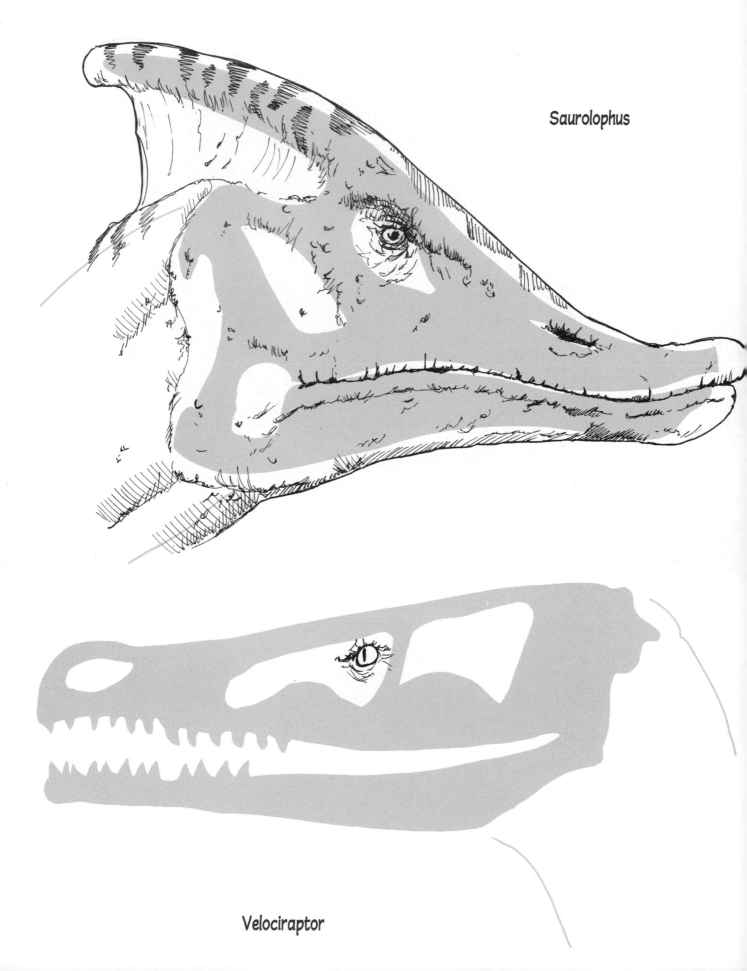

Saurolophus

Velociraptor

Using these skulls to help you, imagine what these dinosaurs' faces looked like.

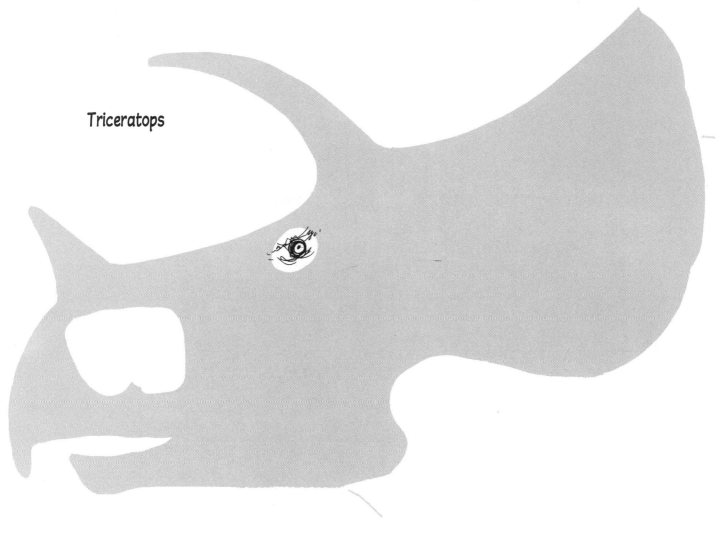

Triceratops

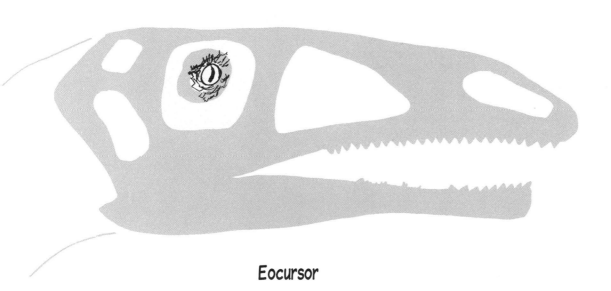

Eocursor

Chindesaurus was a dinosaur that ate lizards and other small reptiles.

Draw all the small reptiles hiding from it.

Some dinosaurs, such as **Dromiceiomimus**, could run at speeds up to 40 miles an hour.

What is trying to catch this Dromiceiomimus?

Give these dinosaurs skins with bright colors and crazy patterns.

Titanosaurus

Australovenator

Draw the bones of their skeletons.

Tltanosaurus

Australovenator

Therizinosaurus had claws that were almost two feet long and very useful for fighting.

Draw a Therizinosaurus about to attack
the dinosaur below.

Stegosaurus had two rows of big bone plates on its back, which may have helped control its body temperature.

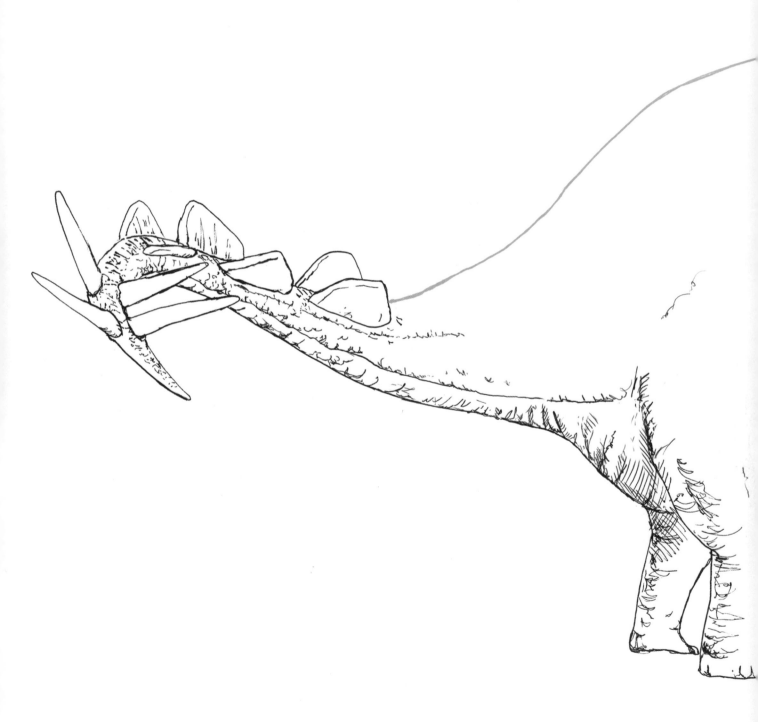

It also had the smallest brain of all the dinosaurs.

Finish the two rows of bone plates on this Stegosaurus.

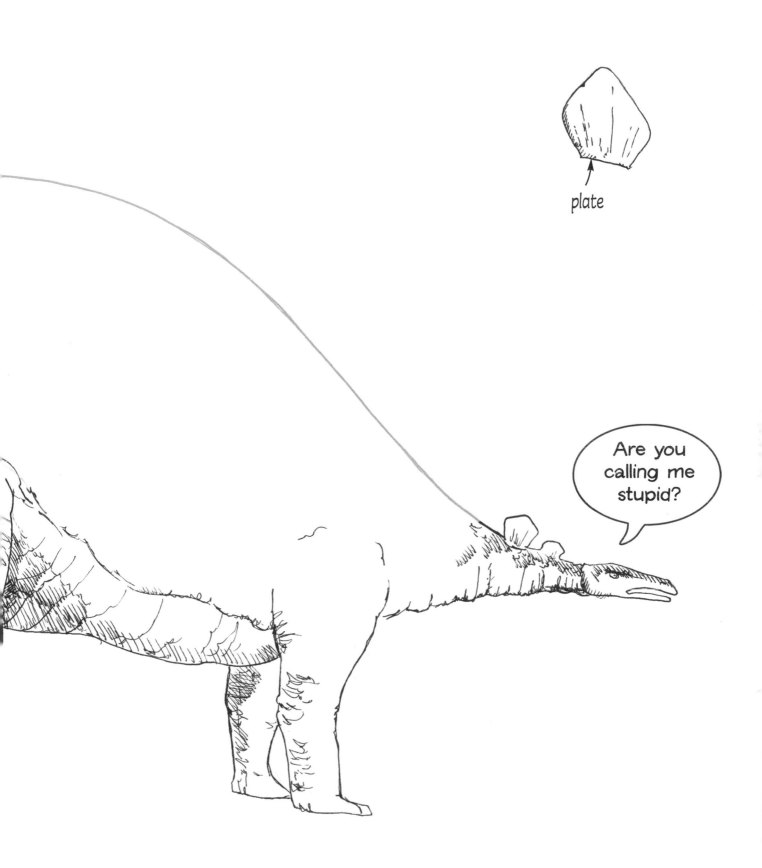

plate

Are you calling me stupid?

This is a **Ceratops** and its babies. Draw some more babies hatching out of eggs and others playing.

At the time of the dinosaurs, the skies were full of flying reptiles known as **pterosaurs**.

Fill this scene with them.

Charming!

Pachycephalosaurus had a thick bony skull and may have butted heads with other dinosaurs.

Draw the other Pachycephalosaurus in this head-butting competition.

Sauropods lived in large herds.

Fill the landscape with sauropods.

Only the bones of dinosaurs remain,
so we don't know what their skin was like.

Draw crazy, colorful patterns on the skins
of these dinosaurs.

One of the scariest dinosaurs was **Utahraptor**. It was very big and fast, with huge claws.

I'm off!

Can you design an even scarier dinosaur?

Draw lots of dinosaurs drinking at this pool . . .

It's busy around here.

. . . and some other creatures in the water, too.

Some dinosaurs, such as **Oryctodromeus**,
lived in burrows. Fill this burrow with dinosaurs.

Gulp! It's dark
down here.

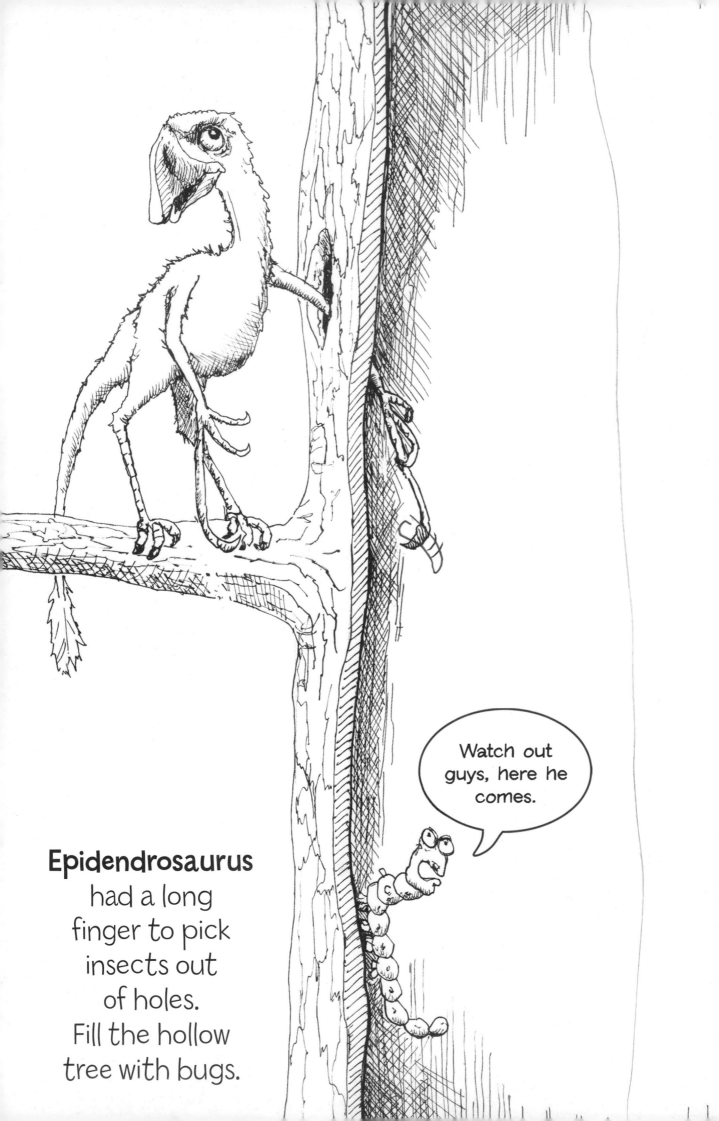

Epidendrosaurus had a long finger to pick insects out of holes. Fill the hollow tree with bugs.

Archaeopteryx was a dinosaur with feathers,
but it probably couldn't fly very well.
Give this one colorful feathers.

Plateosaurus may have been covered in scales.

Cover these two with scales.

Finish the forest and fill it with dinosaurs.

What has frightened this **T-rex**?

Small meat-eating dinosaurs called **Velociraptors** hunted in packs.

Draw a pack of them hunting this dinosaur.

Dinosaurs were in danger from huge crocodiles
that lived in rivers.

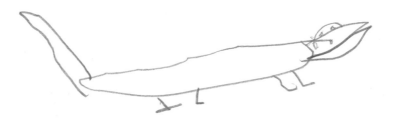

Protoceratops

Velociraptor

These are the two dinosaurs
that were fighting.

Can you draw a cartoon of the two
dinosaurs fighting in these boxes?

5

6

Avalanche!

Some dinosaur fossils have been found in the frozen land of Antarctica, though it was warmer then and had forests.

One was a big meat-eating dinosaur called **Cryolophosaurus**. It is also known as "Elvisaurus" because it had a crest like Elvis' hair.

Another was a plant-eating dinosaur called **Leaellynasaura**. Draw lots of them.

The longest dinosaur ever found is **Seismosaurus**.
It measured up to 150 feet long.

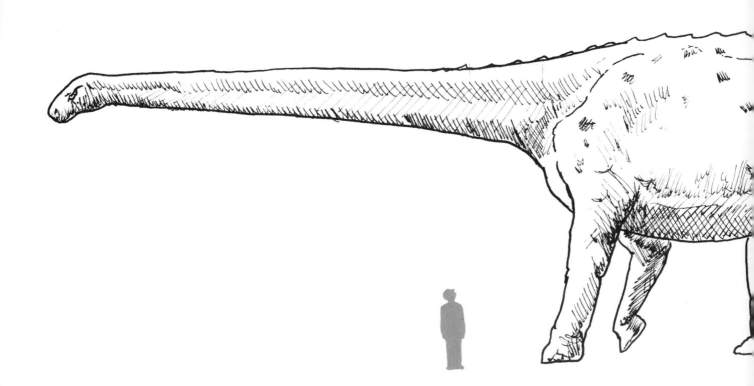

Draw something as long as a Seismosaurus.

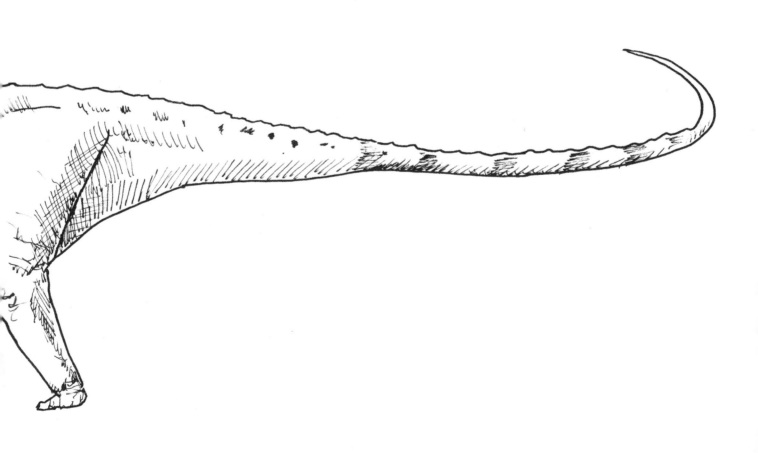

Diplodocus had a very long neck and ate tall trees.

Brachytrachelopan was a short-necked dinosaur that ate bushes and small trees. Draw some of them munching the small trees below.

Minmi was a little dinosaur with thick armor.

Can you design armor for this dinosaur
so that nothing can eat it?

Giganotosaurus looked a bit like T-rex, but it was even bigger!

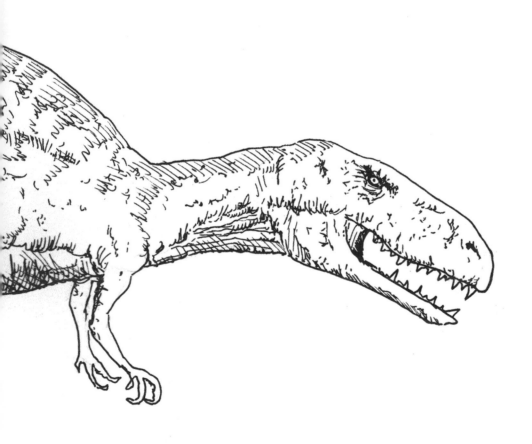

Draw a gigantic Giganotosaurus.

Baryonyx caught fish to eat with its huge claws.
Fill the river with tasty fish.

Raptorex kriegsteini looked exactly the same as a T-rex, but it was only as big as a man.

What is this one attacking?

Majungasaurus was sometimes a "cannibal," which means it ate others of its own kind.

Can you draw the Majungasaurus this one is chasing?

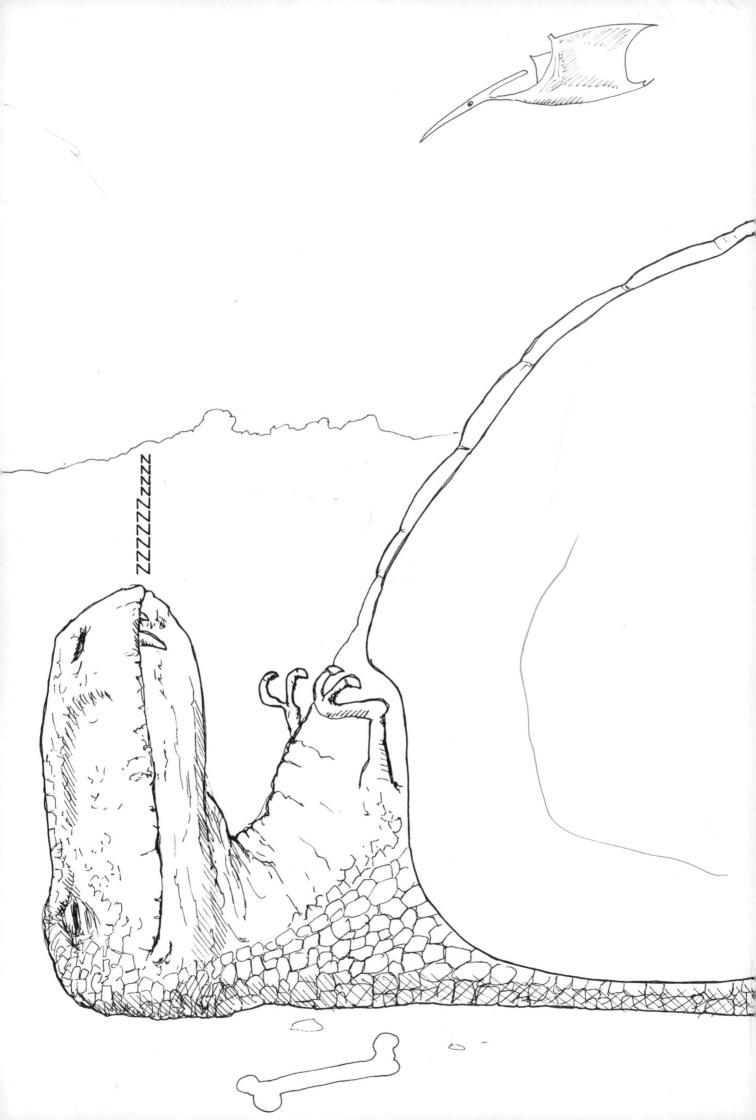

What has this **T-rex** eaten?

Spinosaurus was the biggest meat-eating dinosaur. Some scientists think it had a big sail on its back, but others think it had a big hump, like a buffalo.

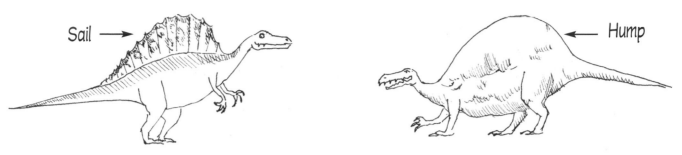

Sail →

← Hump

Finish this one's back any way you like.

Using these skulls to help you, draw their faces.

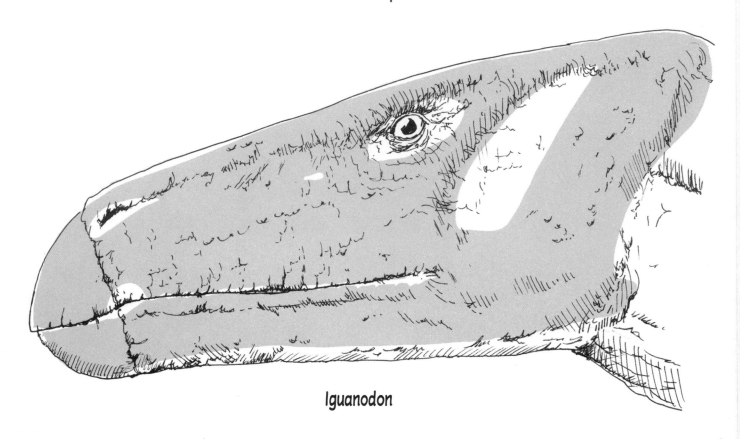

Iguanodon

Tyrannosaurus

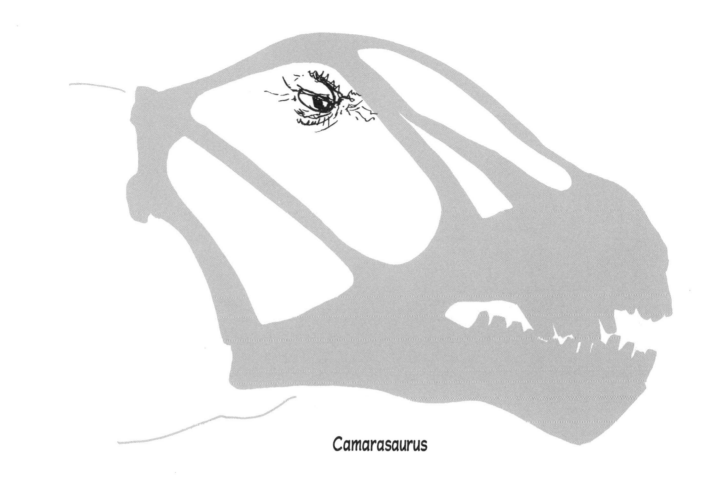

Camarasaurus

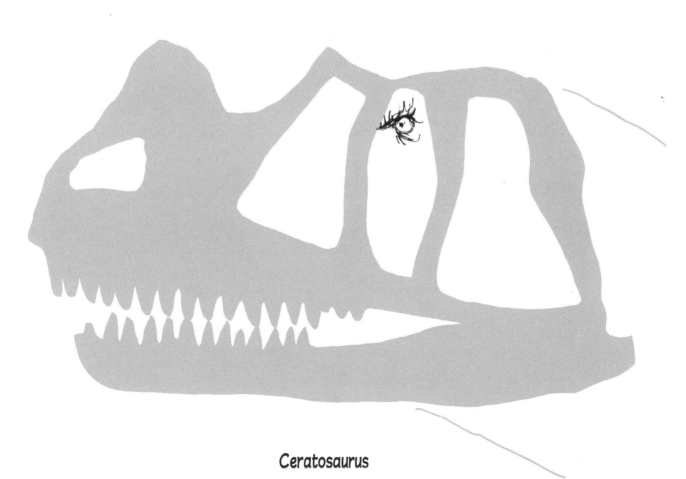

Ceratosaurus

Pinacosaurus had a big, heavy club on its tail,
which it used as a weapon.

Which dinosaur has this Pinacosaurus clubbed?

THWACK!

A small pterosaur called **Anurognathus** may have eaten the insects that lived on dinosaurs' skins or on their feathers.

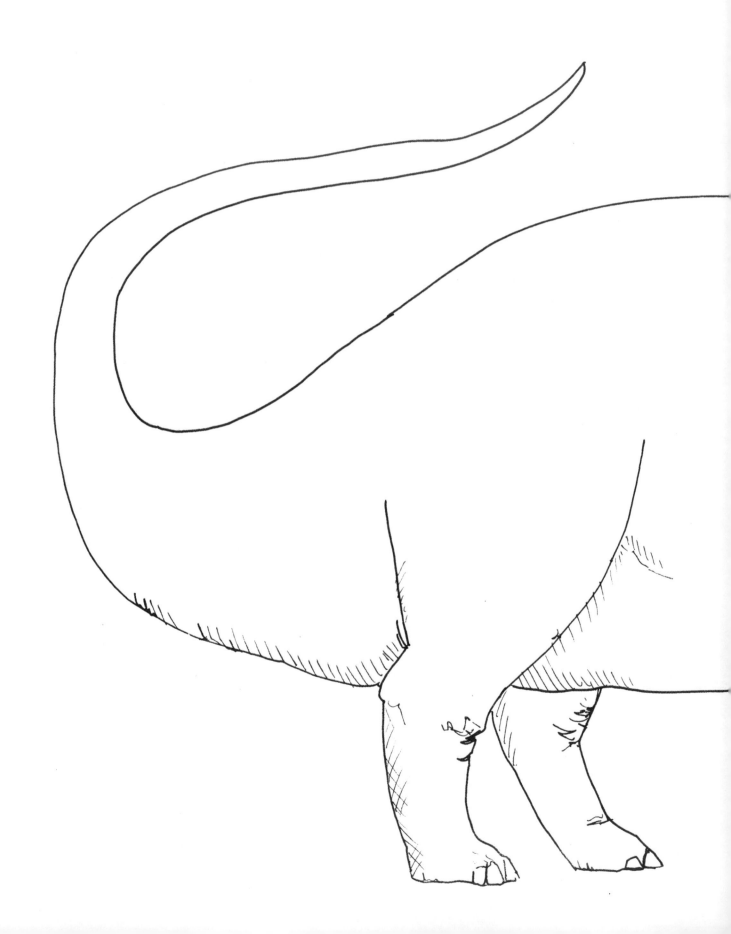

Draw some cleaning this **sauropod.**

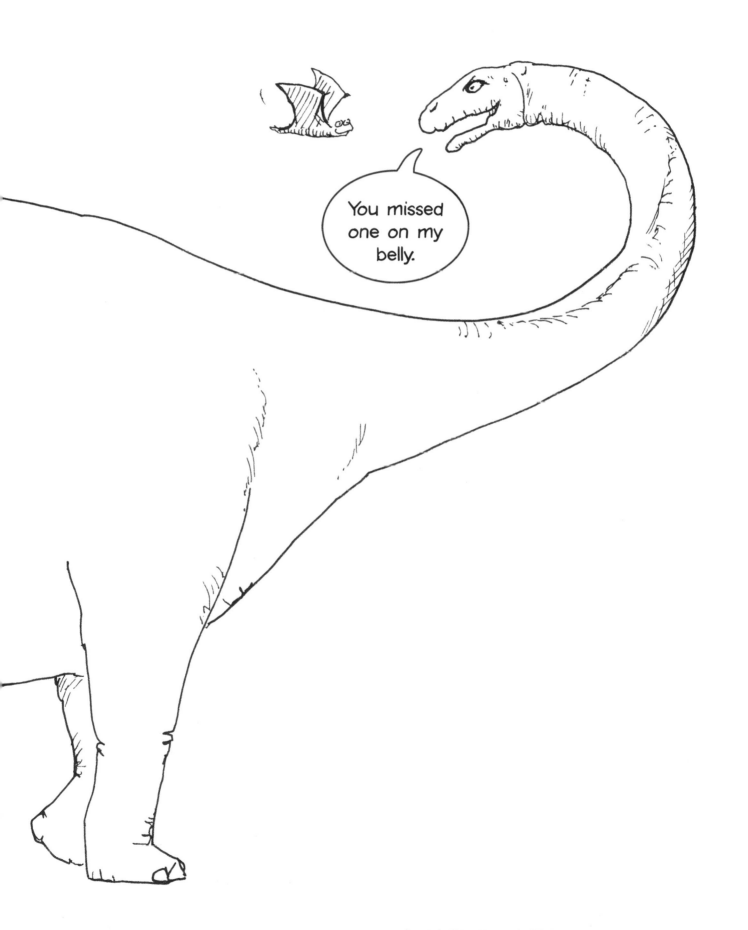

Buitreraptor was a tiny, meat-eating dinosaur that lived alongside Giganotosaurus.

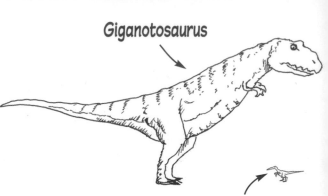

Giganotosaurus

Buitreraptor

Draw a Giganotosaurus arguing with this Buitreraptor.

Tanystropheus was a reptile with a very, very long neck, which it used to catch fish. Fill the sea with fish for it to catch.

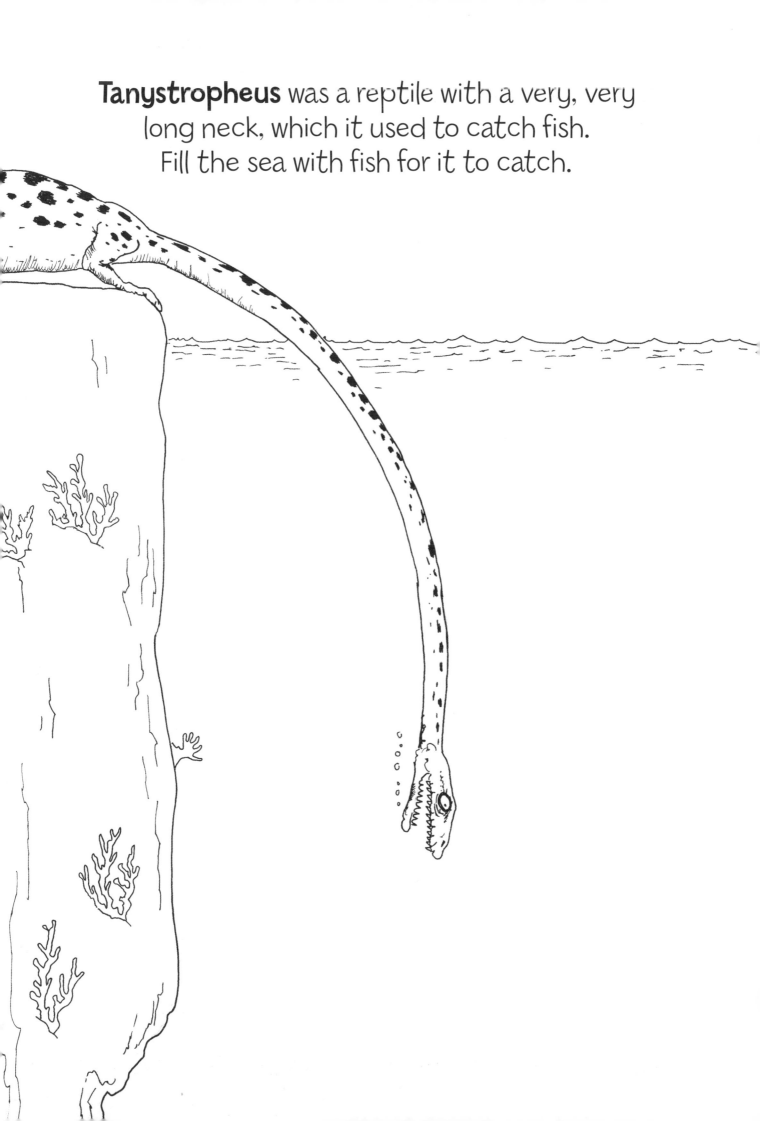

Archaeornithomimus was an "omnivore," which means it ate anything it could find, including the eggs of other dinosaurs.

Quickly draw a mother dinosaur to protect these eggs
from this cheeky Archaeornithomimus.

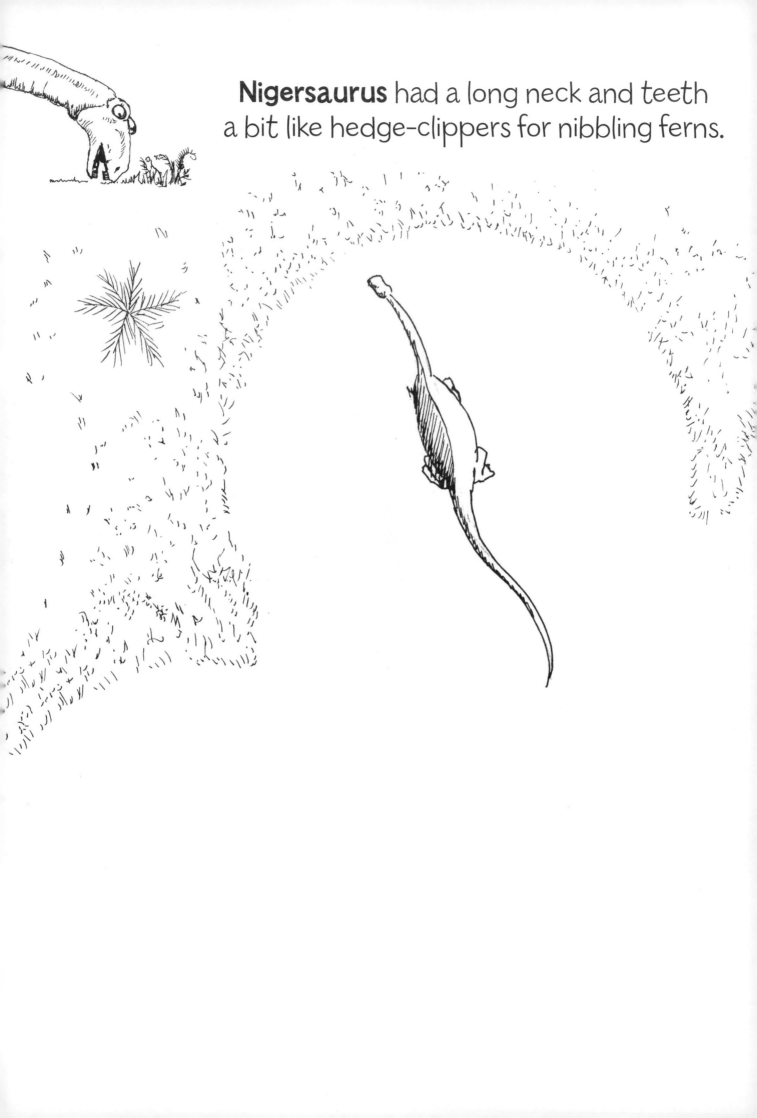

Nigersaurus had a long neck and teeth a bit like hedge-clippers for nibbling ferns.

Draw more of them eating these ferns.

Draw some skin on these dinosaurs.

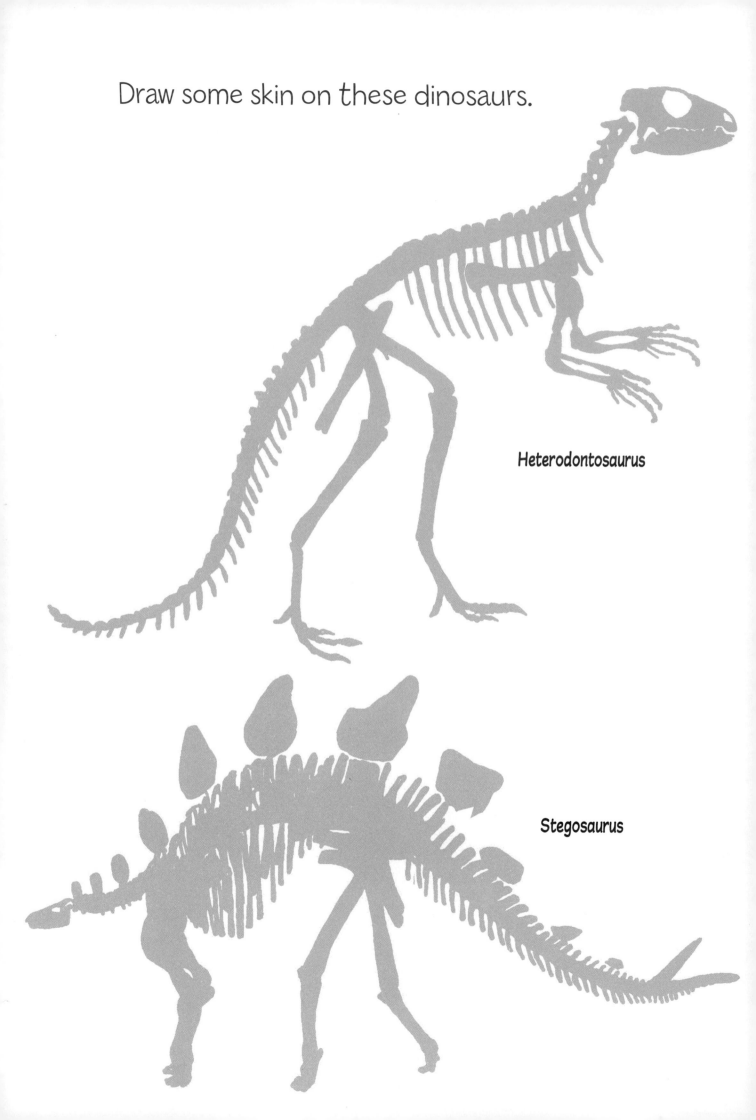

Heterodontosaurus

Stegosaurus

Draw their bones.

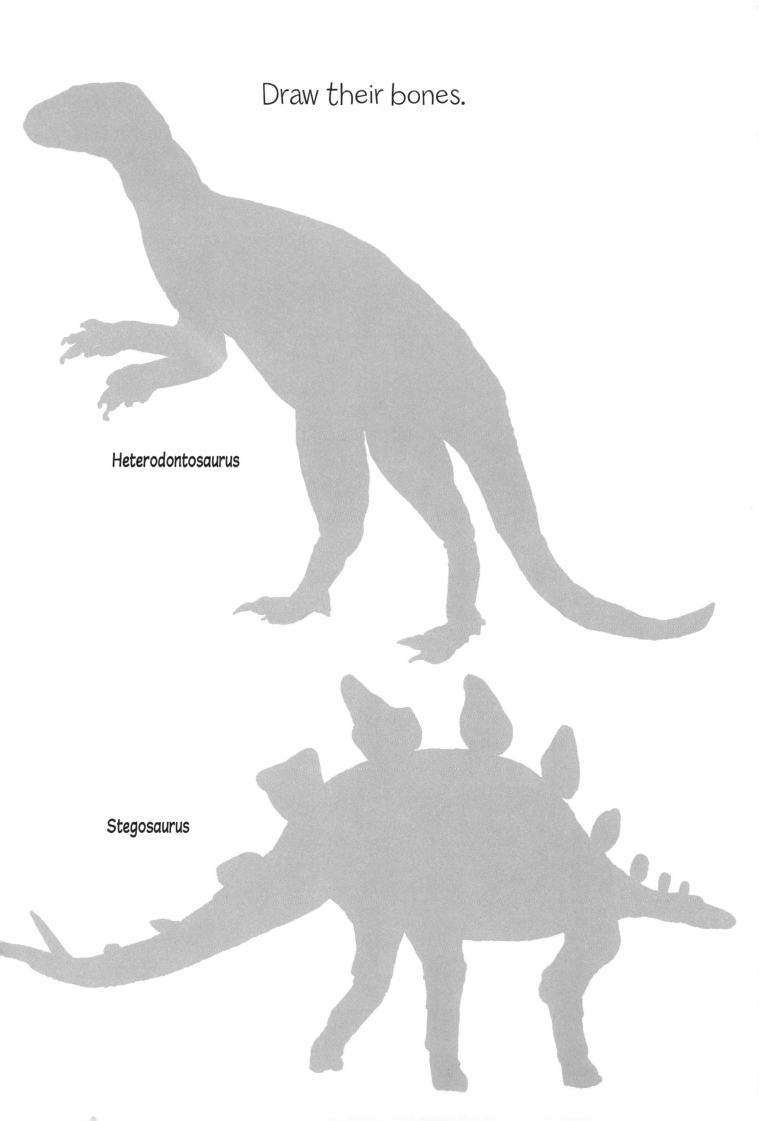

Heterodontosaurus

Stegosaurus

Chirostenotes had a big, bony crest on its head and it probably had feathers.

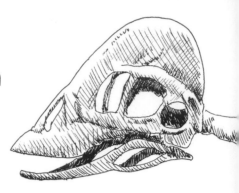

What do you think its head looked like?

Carnotaurus was a big, meat-eating dinosaur with weedy arms. Scientists think it may have eaten dead animals, like vultures do today.

Draw a Carnotaurus eating this dinosaur.

A baby **T-rex** was born covered
in fluff to keep it warm.

Draw some fluffy babies.

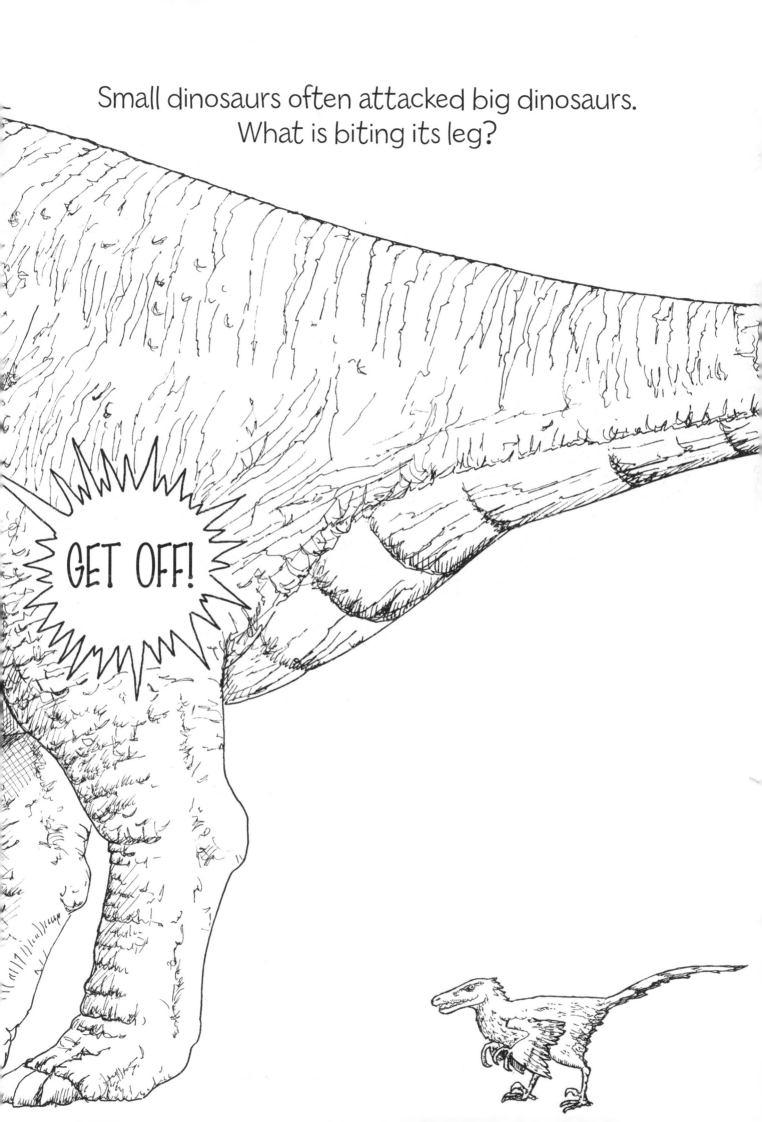

Paleontogolists found the whole skeleton of **Mei Long** (which means "soundly sleeping dragon"). It must have been sleeping when it was buried in mud.

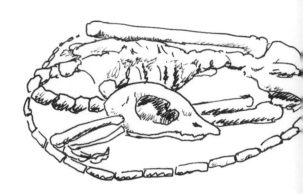

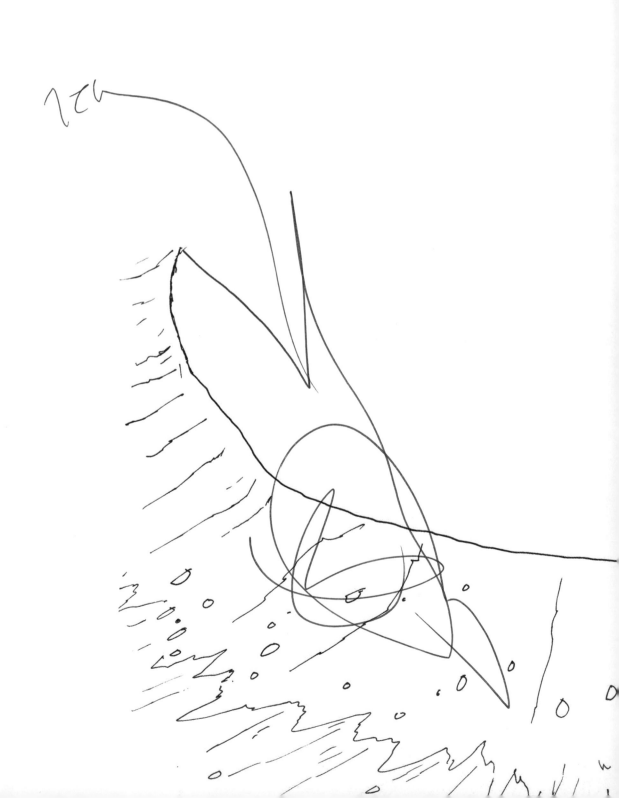

This is what Mei Long looked like. Can you draw one sleeping in the nest below?

Scientists think that a dinosaur known as **Arenysaurus Ardevoli** swam between different islands in the sea.

Draw some between these islands.

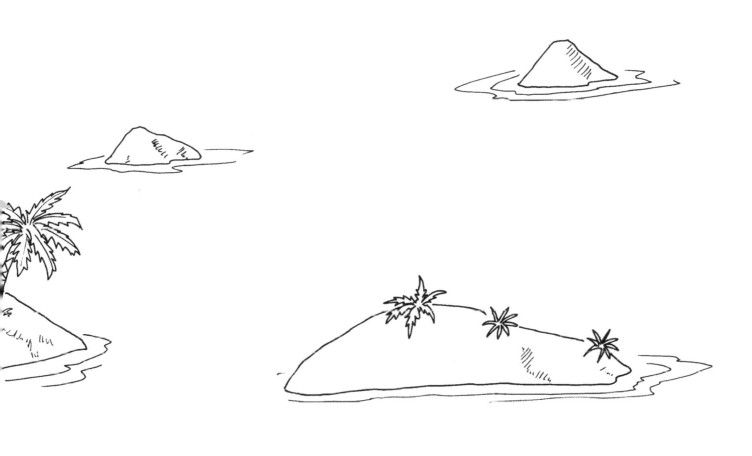

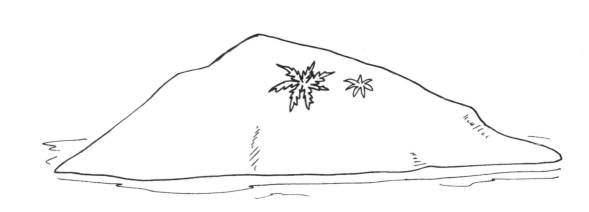

Amargasaurus had two rows of long spikes sticking up from its neck and back.

Nobody knows if these were sharp horns or held colorful sails. Doodle what you think Amargasaurus looked like.

Scientists don't know what the skin
of a **Diplodocus** was like.

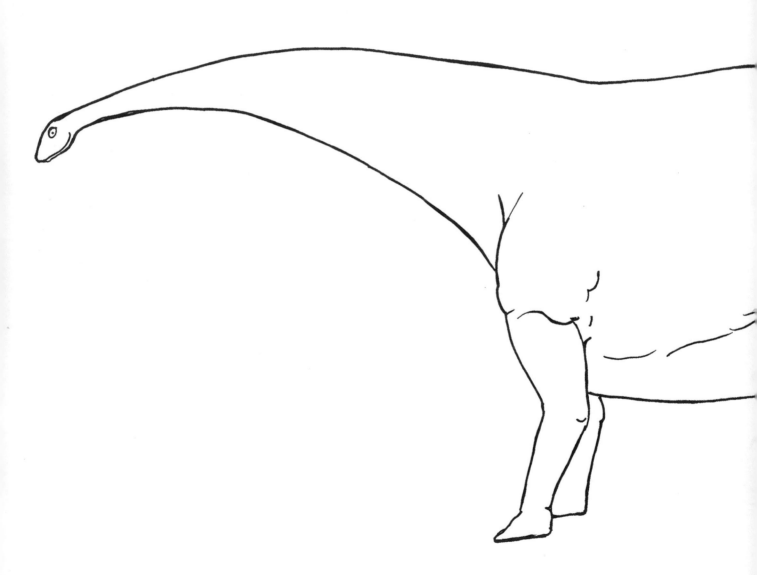

What color and patterns do you think it had?

While dinosaurs ruled the land, the sea was full of huge marine reptiles. Fill this sea with monster reptiles.

What dinosaur is this
creature hiding from?

Parasaurolophus had a crest on its head, which may have helped it to make loud noises. Give the one below a crest, too.

Huge volcanic eruptions may have caused a long, dark winter, which helped to kill off all dinosaurs.

Draw some enormous eruptions, smoke, fire, and lava.

Dinosaurs may have been wiped out when Earth was hit by a huge rock from outer space (called a meteorite).

Draw a meteorite causing a massive, fiery explosion.

Different layers of rock contain different fossils.

Fill these layers with fossils.

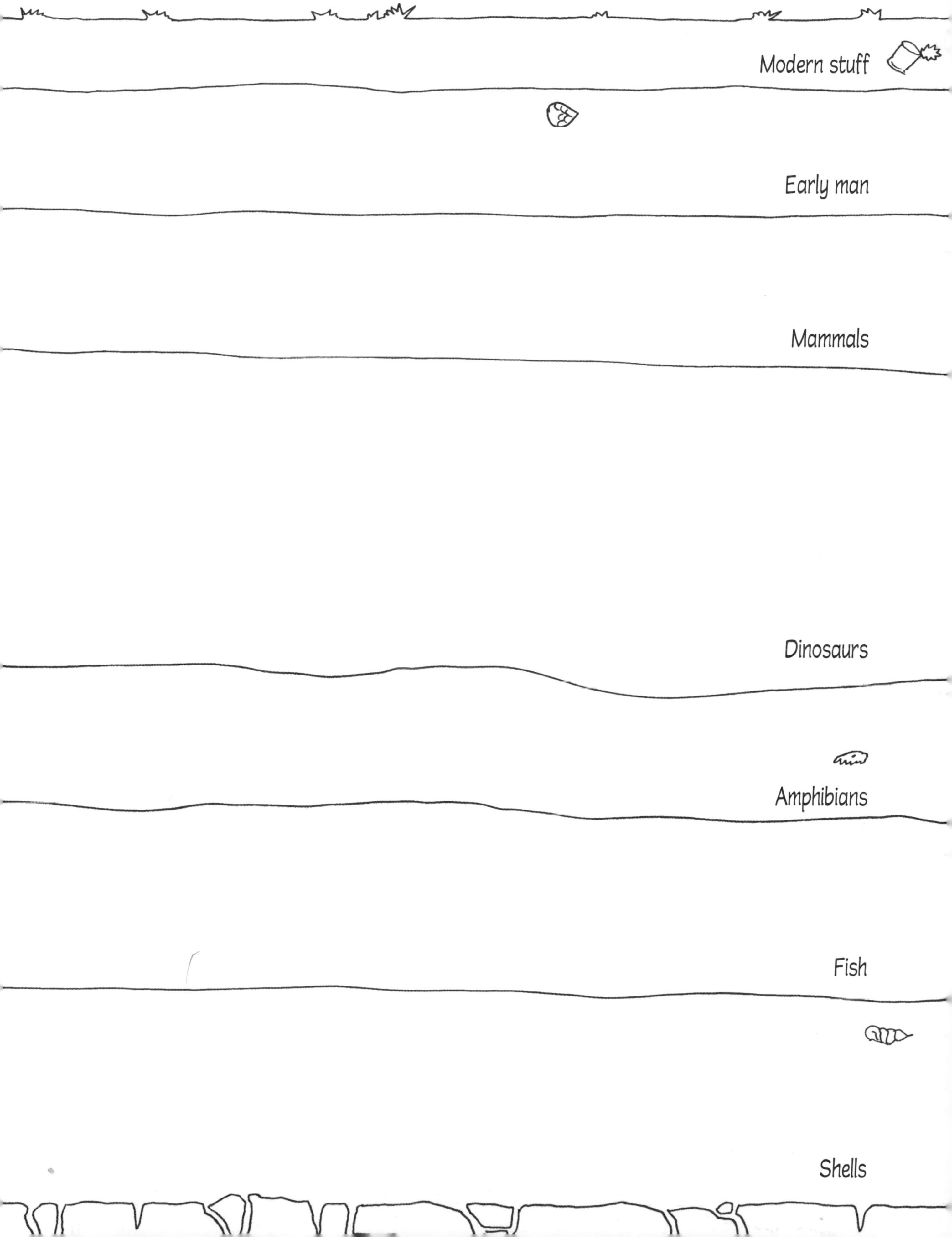

Modern stuff

Early man

Mammals

Dinosaurs

Amphibians

Fish

Shells

People who study fossils are called "paleontologists."

Help this paleontologist complete this skeleton.

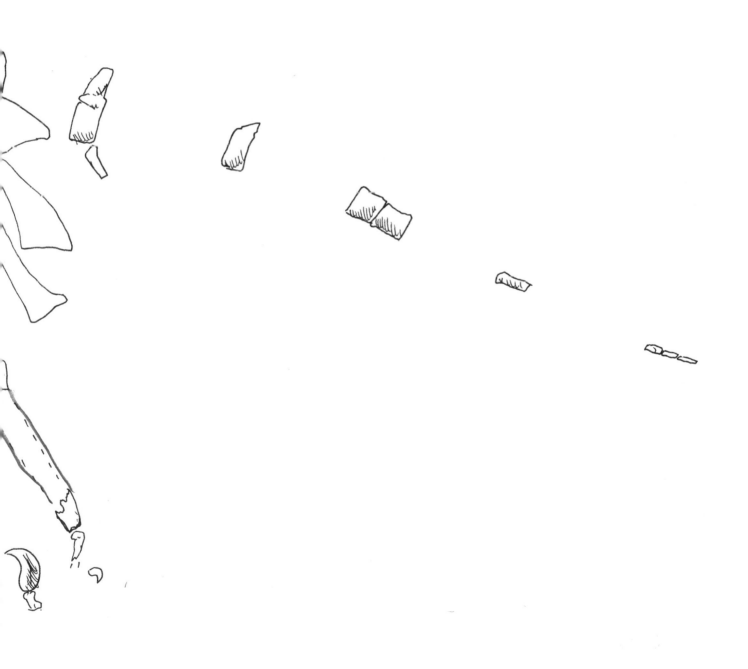

An eight-year-old boy
discovered the fossil
of **Zuniceratops.**

Can you imagine what the fossil looked like?

Imagine if explorers found dinosaurs
still living on Earth . . .

If dinosaurs still existed today,
they might wear clothes and
live in houses.

What do you think they would look like?

In fact, dinosaurs didn't die out altogether.
Some are around today. We call them birds.

Fill the sky with birds.

Fill this page with trails of dinosaur footprints.